100 DAYS TO KILL

Writing Effective Copy to kill your competitor's ranking

KHAIRUL HILMI SIDEK

Copyright © 2024 KHAIRUL HILMI SIDEK

All rights reserved

The characters and events portrayed in this book are fictitious. Any similarity to real persons, living or dead, is coincidental and not intended by the author.

No part of this book may be reproduced, or stored in a retrieval system, or transmitted in any form or by any means, electronic, mechanical, photocopying, recording, or otherwise, without express written permission of the publisher.

INTRODUCTION

"Make it simple. Make it memorable. Make it inviting to look at."
– Leo Burnett

Writing a good content is hard but what is the purpose if people are not attracted to read your content. You can write thousands of articles but is it worth reading?

That is the main purpose of copywriting. How to attract people to act. Either to buy, to search, to ask or to read further.

This book will provide 100 different ways to write a better copy to kill your competitor's ranking.

You can divide the pages into 100 different sheets, print them and read them page by page. In 100 days, you will become an expert of copywriting in whatever writing medium you work on.

This book is designed to be a simple, quick, straight to the point 100 chapters of copywriting success formula.

CONTENTS

Title Page

Copyright

Introduction

DAY 1: Key Elements of an Impactful Home Page	1
DAY 2: Crafting Compelling Headlines	3
DAY 3: The Role of a Clear and Concise Value Proposition	5
DAY 4: Engaging About Us Page	7
DAY 5: Creating Effective Call-to-Actions (CTAs)	9
DAY 6: Optimizing Web Copy for SEO	11
DAY 7: Using Customer Testimonials Effectively	13
DAY 8: Writing Persuasive Product Descriptions	15
DAY 9: The Importance of Consistent Tone and Voice	17
DAY 10: Crafting Engaging Blog Posts	19
DAY 11: Writing Clear and Concise FAQ Sections	21
DAY 12: Leveraging Social Proof in Your Copy	23
DAY 13: How to Write for Your Target Audience	25
DAY 14: Structuring Your Content for Readability	27
DAY 15: Utilizing Data and Statistics in Copy	29
DAY 16: Crafting Effective Meta Descriptions	31
DAY 17: Creating Compelling Landing Pages	33
DAY 18: Writing Effective Email Campaigns	35

DAY 19: Incorporating Storytelling in Your Copy	37
DAY 20: The Role of Visuals in Copywriting	39
DAY 21: Writing for Different Stages of the Buyer's Journey	41
DAY 22: The Importance of A/B Testing Your Copy	43
DAY 23: Copywriting for E-commerce Websites	45
DAY 24: Writing for Mobile Users	47
DAY 25: Writing Effective About Us Pages	49
DAY 26: Creating High-Converting CTAs	51
DAY 27: The Power of Headlines	53
DAY 28: Creating Content that Converts	55
DAY 29: The Impact of User-Generated Content	57
DAY 30: Writing for Different Platforms	59
DAY 31: Crafting Clear and Compelling Offers	61
DAY 32: Writing for B2B Audiences	63
DAY 33: The Role of Emotions in Copywriting	65
DAY 34: Writing for SEO	67
DAY 35: Writing Effective Blog Posts	69
DAY 36: The Importance of Proofreading and Editing	71
DAY 37: Copywriting Trends to Watch	73
DAY 38: Writing for Different Industries	75
DAY 39: Effective Copywriting for Social Media Ads	77
DAY 40: Writing Persuasive Product Descriptions	79
DAY 41: Enhancing Copy with Interactive Elements	81
DAY 42: Crafting Compelling Brand Stories	83
DAY 43: Writing for Video Scripts	85
DAY 44: Writing Engaging Email Subject Lines	87
DAY 45: The Role of Consistency in Copywriting	89
DAY 46: Leveraging User Feedback in Copywriting	91

DAY 47: Writing for Global Audiences	93
DAY 48: Writing for Different Generations	95
DAY 49: Writing Compelling Case Studies	97
DAY 50: The Power of Storytelling in Copywriting	99
DAY 51: Writing for Voice Search	101
DAY 52: Writing for Email Marketing	103
DAY 53: The Importance of Visual Copywriting	105
DAY 54: Writing for Different Content Formats	107
DAY 55: Writing Engaging Webinar Content	109
DAY 56: Writing for Product Launches	111
DAY 57: Writing for Nonprofit Organizations	113
DAY 58: Writing for Event Promotion	115
DAY 59: Writing for Online Courses	117
DAY 60: Writing for Crowdfunding Campaigns	119
DAY 61: Writing for Podcasts	121
DAY 62: Writing for Video Marketing	123
DAY 63: Writing for Print Advertising	125
DAY 64: Writing for Influencer Marketing	127
DAY 65: Writing for Crisis Communication	129
DAY 66: Writing for Landing Pages	131
DAY 67: Writing for User Onboarding	133
DAY 68: Writing for Customer Retention	135
DAY 69: Writing for Surveys and Feedback Forms	137
DAY 70: Writing for SEO	139
DAY 71: Writing for E-commerce	141
DAY 72: Writing for Sales Pages	143
DAY 73: Writing for Educational Content	145
DAY 74: Writing for Healthcare	147

DAY 75: Writing for Finance	149
DAY 76: Writing for Technology	151
DAY 77: Writing for Travel	153
DAY 78: Writing for Lifestyle	155
DAY 79: Writing for Sports	157
DAY 80: Writing for Real Estate	159
DAY 81: Writing for B2B	161
DAY 82: Writing for B2C	163
DAY 83: Writing for Nonprofits	165
DAY 84: Writing for Internal Communications	167
DAY 85: Writing for Academic Content	169
DAY 86: Writing for Legal Content	171
DAY 87: Writing for Event Promotion	173
DAY 88: Writing for Press Releases	175
DAY 89: Writing for Email Newsletters	177
DAY 90: Writing for Social Media	179
DAY 91: Writing for Blogs	181
DAY 92: Writing for Video Scripts REVISITED	183
DAY 93: Writing for Podcasts REVISITED	185
DAY 94: Writing for Webinars	187
DAY 95: Writing for Presentations	189
DAY 96: Strategies for Increasing Email Open Rates	191
DAY 97: Writing for Voice Search	193
DAY 98: The Future of Copywriting	195
DAY 99: Writing for Global Audiences	197
DAY 100: Continuous Learning and Improvement	199
Conclusion	201

DAY 1: KEY ELEMENTS OF AN IMPACTFUL HOME PAGE

An impactful home page is crucial for capturing the attention of visitors and encouraging them to explore your website further. Here are the key elements that should be included:

1. **Clear Value Proposition**: Communicate what your business offers and why it's valuable.
2. **Engaging Headline**: Use a compelling headline that draws visitors in and encourages them to read more.
3. **Visual Appeal**: Incorporate high-quality images or videos that are relevant to your business.
4. **User-Friendly Navigation**: Ensure that the navigation menu is easy to use and helps visitors find what they need quickly.
5. **Call-to-Action (CTA)**: Include clear and compelling CTAs to guide visitors towards taking desired actions.
6. **Social Proof**: Add testimonials, reviews, or case studies to build trust and credibility.
7. **Contact Information**: Make it easy for visitors to get in

touch with you by including your contact information prominently.

8. **Responsive Design**: Ensure that your home page is optimized for different devices, including mobile phones and tablets.
9. **Fast Load Time**: Optimize your home page to load quickly, as slow load times can deter visitors.
10. **SEO Elements**: Incorporate keywords, meta tags, and other SEO best practices to improve your search engine ranking.

DAY 2: CRAFTING COMPELLING HEADLINES

Headlines are one of the most critical components of your web copy. They determine whether a visitor will read the rest of your content or move on. Here are some tips for crafting compelling headlines:

1. **Be Clear and Specific**: Clearly state what the reader will gain from reading your content.
2. **Use Numbers and Lists**: Headlines with numbers or lists often perform better as they promise specific information.
3. **Create a Sense of Urgency**: Use words that create a sense of urgency or importance.
4. **Ask Questions**: Asking a question can engage readers and prompt them to seek the answer in your content.
5. **Use Power Words**: Incorporate powerful, emotion-evoking words to grab attention.
6. **Keep It Short and Sweet**: Aim for headlines that are concise yet informative.
7. **Test Different Headlines**: A/B test different headlines

to see which ones perform best.
8. **Highlight Benefits**: Focus on the benefits that the reader will get from your content.
9. **Incorporate Keywords**: Use relevant keywords to improve SEO and ensure the headline is relevant to the content.
10. **Be Honest**: Ensure that the headline accurately reflects the content to avoid misleading readers.

DAY 3: THE ROLE OF A CLEAR AND CONCISE VALUE PROPOSITION

A value proposition is a statement that explains what makes your product or service unique and why customers should choose you over the competition. Here's how to create a clear and concise value proposition:

1. **Identify Your Unique Selling Points (USPs)**: Determine what sets your business apart from competitors.
2. **Understand Your Target Audience**: Know who your customers are and what they value.
3. **Focus on Benefits**: Highlight the benefits and value your product or service provides.
4. **Be Specific**: Avoid vague statements and be specific about what you offer.
5. **Use Simple Language**: Ensure your value proposition is easy to understand.
6. **Make It Memorable**: Craft a value proposition that is catchy and easy to remember.
7. **Test and Refine**: Test different value propositions to

see which resonates most with your audience.
8. **Incorporate Social Proof**: Use testimonials or case studies to back up your value proposition.
9. **Highlight Pain Points**: Address the specific problems or needs of your target audience.
10. **Ensure Visibility**: Place your value proposition prominently on your home page and other key areas of your website.

DAY 4: ENGAGING ABOUT US PAGE

An engaging About Us page helps build a connection with your audience by telling your brand's story and establishing trust. Here's how to create one:

1. **Share Your Story**: Tell the story of how your business started and what drives you.
2. **Highlight Your Mission and Values**: Communicate your mission, values, and what you stand for.
3. **Showcase Your Team**: Introduce the people behind the brand with photos and short bios.
4. **Incorporate Visuals**: Use images or videos to make the page more engaging.
5. **Include Testimonials**: Add testimonials or quotes from satisfied customers.
6. **Highlight Achievements**: Mention any awards, recognitions, or significant milestones.
7. **Be Authentic**: Use a tone and language that reflects your brand's personality.
8. **Call to Action**: Include a CTA that guides visitors on what to do next, such as contacting you or learning more about your services.

9. **Make It Easy to Read**: Use headings, bullet points, and short paragraphs for better readability.
10. **Keep It Updated**: Regularly update the page with new information and achievements.

DAY 5: CREATING EFFECTIVE CALL-TO-ACTIONS (CTAS)

Call-to-Actions (CTAs) are essential for guiding visitors towards taking specific actions on your website. Here's how to create effective CTAs:

1. **Use Action-Oriented Language**: Use verbs and phrases that prompt action, such as "Get Started," "Learn More," or "Sign Up."
2. **Be Clear and Direct**: Ensure that the CTA clearly communicates what the visitor should do next.
3. **Create a Sense of Urgency**: Use phrases like "Limited Time Offer" or "Act Now" to create urgency.
4. **Highlight Benefits**: Make it clear what the visitor will gain by taking action.
5. **Use Contrasting Colors**: Make the CTA button stand out with contrasting colors.
6. **Keep It Short**: Use concise and straightforward language.
7. **Place CTAs Strategically**: Position CTAs where they are easily noticeable, such as above the fold or at the end of

content.
8. **Test Different CTAs**: A/B test different CTAs to determine which ones perform best.
9. **Use Multiple CTAs**: Include CTAs in various sections of your website to capture different types of visitors.
10. **Make It Mobile-Friendly**: Ensure that CTAs are easily clickable on mobile devices.

DAY 6: OPTIMIZING WEB COPY FOR SEO

Optimizing your web copy for search engines is essential for improving visibility and attracting more visitors. Here are some strategies:

1. **Keyword Research**: Identify the keywords your target audience is searching for.
2. **Use Keywords Strategically**: Incorporate keywords naturally into your headings, subheadings, and body text.
3. **Create Quality Content**: Focus on providing valuable, informative, and engaging content.
4. **Optimize Meta Tags**: Write compelling meta titles and descriptions that include your primary keywords.
5. **Use Alt Text for Images**: Describe your images with relevant keywords in the alt text.
6. **Improve Readability**: Use short paragraphs, bullet points, and subheadings to make your content easy to read.
7. **Internal Linking**: Link to other relevant pages on your website to improve navigation and SEO.
8. **Mobile Optimization**: Ensure your website is mobile-friendly to enhance user experience and SEO.

9. **Fast Load Times**: Optimize your website's speed to reduce bounce rates.
10. **Regularly Update Content**: Keep your content fresh and updated to maintain relevance and rankings.

DAY 7: USING CUSTOMER TESTIMONIALS EFFECTIVELY

Customer testimonials are powerful tools for building trust and credibility. Here's how to use them effectively:

1. **Collect Genuine Testimonials**: Request feedback from satisfied customers.
2. **Highlight Specific Benefits**: Use testimonials that mention specific benefits or results.
3. **Include Customer Details**: Add names, photos, and positions to make testimonials more credible.
4. **Use Various Formats**: Incorporate written testimonials, video testimonials, and case studies.
5. **Place Strategically**: Display testimonials on key pages like the home page, product pages, and landing pages.
6. **Update Regularly**: Keep your testimonials

current by adding new ones regularly.
7. **Use Testimonials in Marketing**: Include testimonials in email campaigns, social media posts, and ads.
8. **Create a Dedicated Page**: Have a testimonials or reviews page on your website.
9. **Show Diversity**: Use testimonials from a range of customers to appeal to different audience segments.
10. **Seek Permission**: Always get consent from customers before publishing their testimonials.

DAY 8: WRITING PERSUASIVE PRODUCT DESCRIPTIONS

Effective product descriptions can significantly impact purchasing decisions. Here's how to write persuasive product descriptions:

1. **Focus on Benefits**: Highlight the benefits of the product, not just the features.
2. **Know Your Audience**: Tailor your descriptions to the needs and preferences of your target audience.
3. **Use Sensory Words**: Engage the reader's senses by using descriptive language.
4. **Create a Story**: Tell a story about the product and how it can improve the customer's life.
5. **Use Bullet Points**: List key features and benefits in bullet points for easy scanning.
6. **Incorporate Keywords**: Use relevant keywords for SEO.
7. **Include Social Proof**: Add reviews or ratings to the

product description.
8. **Keep It Concise**: Be clear and concise, avoiding unnecessary information.
9. **Highlight Unique Selling Points (USPs)**: Emphasize what makes the product unique.
10. **Use High-Quality Images**: Complement the description with high-quality images of the product.

DAY 9: THE IMPORTANCE OF CONSISTENT TONE AND VOICE

Maintaining a consistent tone and voice in your web copy is essential for building a strong brand identity. Here's how to achieve it:

1. **Define Your Brand Voice**: Determine your brand's personality and how you want to communicate.
2. **Create a Style Guide**: Develop a style guide that outlines your tone, voice, and writing guidelines.
3. **Know Your Audience**: Tailor your tone and voice to resonate with your target audience.
4. **Be Authentic**: Ensure your tone and voice reflect your brand's values and culture.
5. **Use Consistent Language**: Avoid switching between different styles of writing.
6. **Train Your Team**: Ensure everyone involved in creating content understands and follows the style guide.

7. **Review Regularly**: Regularly review and update your style guide as needed.
8. **Be Adaptable**: While maintaining consistency, adapt your tone and voice to suit different contexts and platforms.
9. **Monitor Feedback**: Pay attention to audience feedback to refine your tone and voice.
10. **Stay True to Your Brand**: Always stay true to your brand's core message and values.

DAY 10: CRAFTING ENGAGING BLOG POSTS

Engaging blog posts can drive traffic to your website and establish you as an authority in your industry. Here's how to craft them:

1. **Choose Relevant Topics**: Select topics that are relevant to your audience and industry.
2. **Create Catchy Headlines**: Write headlines that grab attention and encourage clicks.
3. **Provide Value**: Offer valuable information, tips, or insights that benefit your readers.
4. **Use an Engaging Opening**: Start with a hook that draws readers in.
5. **Structure Your Content**: Use headings, subheadings, and bullet points to organize your content.
6. **Use Visuals**: Incorporate images, infographics, and videos to enhance your content.
7. **Include Internal and External Links**: Link to other relevant content on your website and reputable external sources.

8. **Encourage Interaction**: Ask questions, invite comments, and encourage sharing to engage readers.
9. **Optimize for SEO**: Use keywords, meta tags, and other SEO best practices.
10. **Promote Your Posts:** Share your blog posts on social media and through email newsletters.

DAY 11: WRITING CLEAR AND CONCISE FAQ SECTIONS

FAQs can improve user experience by addressing common questions. Here's how to write effective FAQ sections:

1. **Identify Common Questions**: Gather questions frequently asked by your customers.
2. **Provide Clear Answers**: Offer straightforward and concise answers.
3. **Use Simple Language**: Avoid jargon and complex language.
4. **Organize Logically**: Group related questions and use headings to organize them.
5. **Keep It Updated**: Regularly update your FAQ section with new questions and answers.
6. **Include Search Functionality**: Add a search bar to help users find specific answers quickly.
7. **Use Visuals When Necessary**: Include images or videos to illustrate answers.
8. **Link to Detailed Information**: Provide links to more in-depth articles or resources.

9. **Make It Easy to Find**: Ensure your FAQ section is easily accessible from your main menu.
10. **Monitor and Analyze**: Track which questions are most frequently accessed to refine your content.

DAY 12: LEVERAGING SOCIAL PROOF IN YOUR COPY

Social proof can significantly enhance your copy by building trust and credibility. Here's how to leverage it:

1. **Use Customer Reviews**: Highlight positive reviews from satisfied customers.
2. **Showcase Testimonials**: Include testimonials from well-known clients or industry experts.
3. **Display Ratings**: Feature ratings and star reviews prominently.
4. **Mention Media Mentions**: Highlight any mentions or features in the media.
5. **Showcase User Numbers**: Mention the number of users or customers who have used your product or service.
6. **Use Case Studies**: Provide detailed case studies that demonstrate success stories.
7. **Include Social Media Proof**: Highlight social media engagement, such as likes, shares, and comments.

8. **Use Badges and Certifications**: Display any relevant badges, certifications, or awards.
9. **Show Before-and-After Results**: Use before-and-after images or stories to demonstrate effectiveness.
10. **Encourage User-Generated Content**: Invite customers to share their experiences and feature their content.

DAY 13: HOW TO WRITE FOR YOUR TARGET AUDIENCE

Writing for your target audience ensures that your content resonates with them. Here's how to do it effectively:

1. **Understand Your Audience**: Conduct research to understand your audience's demographics, interests, and pain points.
2. **Create Buyer Personas**: Develop detailed buyer personas to guide your writing.
3. **Use Relevant Language**: Use language and terminology that your audience is familiar with.
4. **Address Pain Points**: Focus on addressing the specific problems and needs of your audience.
5. **Provide Value**: Offer information, tips, and solutions that are valuable to your audience.
6. **Engage Emotionally**: Connect with your audience on an emotional level.
7. **Use Stories**: Tell stories that your audience can relate to.

8. **Be Authentic**: Write in a way that is genuine and true to your brand.
9. **Encourage Interaction**: Invite your audience to engage with your content through comments and shares.
10. **Analyze Feedback**: Regularly review feedback and adjust your writing to better meet your audience's needs.

DAY 14: STRUCTURING YOUR CONTENT FOR READABILITY

Readable content keeps visitors engaged and improves their experience. Here's how to structure your content:

1. **Use Headings and Subheadings**: Break up your content with clear headings and subheadings.
2. **Keep Paragraphs Short**: Use short paragraphs to make your content easier to read.
3. **Use Bullet Points and Lists**: Use bullet points and lists to highlight key points.
4. **Incorporate Visuals**: Use images, infographics, and videos to break up text and add interest.
5. **Use White Space**: Ensure there is plenty of white space to prevent your content from looking cluttered.
6. **Highlight Important Information**: Use bold or italics to emphasize key points.
7. **Use Simple Language**: Avoid complex words

and jargon.
8. **Write in an Active Voice**: Use an active voice to make your writing more direct and engaging.
9. **Include Summaries**: Provide summaries or key takeaways for longer content.
10. **Test Readability**: Use readability tools to ensure your content is easy to read.

DAY 15: UTILIZING DATA AND STATISTICS IN COPY

Using data and statistics can strengthen your copy by adding credibility and supporting your claims. Here's how to do it effectively:

1. **Use Relevant Data**: Include data that is relevant to your topic and audience.
2. **Source Credible Data**: Use data from reputable and reliable sources.
3. **Present Data Clearly**: Use charts, graphs, and infographics to present data clearly.
4. **Integrate Data Seamlessly**: Integrate data into your copy naturally without overwhelming the reader.
5. **Highlight Key Statistics**: Use bold or callouts to emphasize important statistics.
6. **Provide Context**: Explain the significance of the data and how it supports your points.
7. **Keep It Updated**: Ensure your data is current and reflects the latest information.
8. **Use Comparative Data**: Show comparisons to

highlight trends and differences.
9. **Avoid Overloading with Data**: Use data sparingly to avoid overwhelming your audience.
10. **Cite Your Sources**: Always credit the sources of your data.

DAY 16: CRAFTING EFFECTIVE META DESCRIPTIONS

Meta descriptions are crucial for attracting clicks from search engine results pages. Here's how to craft effective meta descriptions:

1. **Keep It Concise**: Aim for around 150-160 characters.
2. **Include Keywords**: Use relevant keywords naturally.
3. **Be Compelling**: Write a description that entices users to click.
4. **Highlight Benefits**: Emphasize what users will gain from visiting your page.
5. **Use Active Language**: Use action-oriented language.
6. **Match the Content**: Ensure the meta description accurately reflects the content of the page.
7. **Avoid Duplicate Descriptions**: Create unique descriptions for each page.
8. **Use a Call to Action**: Include a CTA to encourage clicks.
9. **Test and Refine**: Test different meta descriptions to see which perform best.
10. **Monitor Performance**: Use analytics to track the

performance of your meta descriptions.

DAY 17: CREATING COMPELLING LANDING PAGES

Landing pages are designed to convert visitors into leads or customers. Here's how to create compelling landing pages:

1. **Focus on a Single Goal**: Each landing page should have one clear goal or CTA.
2. **Craft a Strong Headline**: Use a headline that grabs attention and clearly conveys the value proposition.
3. **Use Engaging Visuals**: Incorporate images or videos that support your message.
4. **Provide Social Proof**: Include testimonials, reviews, or case studies.
5. **Highlight Benefits**: Clearly state the benefits of your offer.
6. **Use a Clear CTA**: Make your CTA button prominent and clear.
7. **Keep It Simple**: Avoid clutter and keep the page focused on the main goal.
8. **Optimize for Mobile**: Ensure your landing page is

mobile-friendly.
9. **Use A/B Testing**: Test different versions of your landing page to optimize performance.
10. **Track Conversions**: Use analytics to track the effectiveness of your landing page.

DAY 18: WRITING EFFECTIVE EMAIL CAMPAIGNS

Email campaigns can drive engagement and conversions. Here's how to write effective email campaigns:

1. **Craft a Compelling Subject Line**: Use a subject line that grabs attention and entices opens.
2. **Personalize Your Emails**: Use the recipient's name and tailor content to their interests.
3. **Keep It Short and Sweet**: Be concise and get to the point quickly.
4. **Use a Clear CTA**: Include a clear and compelling CTA.
5. **Provide Value**: Offer valuable content, such as tips, discounts, or exclusive offers.
6. **Use Engaging Visuals**: Incorporate images, GIFs, or videos to make your emails more engaging.
7. **Segment Your Audience**: Send targeted emails to different segments of your audience.
8. **Test and Optimize**: A/B test different elements

of your emails to optimize performance.
9. **Monitor Metrics**: Track open rates, click-through rates, and conversions to measure success.
10. **Maintain Consistency**: Ensure your emails are consistent with your brand's tone and style.

DAY 19: INCORPORATING STORYTELLING IN YOUR COPY

Storytelling can make your copy more engaging and memorable. Here's how to incorporate storytelling effectively:

1. **Know Your Audience**: Understand what resonates with your audience.
2. **Create a Relatable Hero**: Use a protagonist that your audience can relate to.
3. **Build a Narrative Arc**: Structure your story with a beginning, middle, and end.
4. **Use Emotion**: Engage your audience's emotions through your story.
5. **Highlight a Conflict**: Introduce a challenge or problem that needs to be resolved.
6. **Show Transformation**: Demonstrate how your product or service brings about positive change.
7. **Use Descriptive Language**: Use vivid descriptions to

paint a picture.
8. **Be Authentic**: Ensure your story is genuine and true to your brand.
9. **Incorporate Testimonials**: Use customer stories and testimonials to add authenticity.
10. **Keep It Relevant**: Ensure your story aligns with your overall message and goals.

DAY 20: THE ROLE OF VISUALS IN COPYWRITING

Visuals can enhance your copy and make it more engaging. Here's how to effectively use visuals in copywriting:

1. **Use High-Quality Images**: Incorporate high-resolution, professional images.
2. **Include Infographics**: Use infographics to present data and information visually.
3. **Incorporate Videos**: Use videos to explain complex concepts or showcase products.
4. **Use Illustrations**: Use custom illustrations to add a unique touch.
5. **Optimize for Load Time**: Ensure visuals do not slow down your website.
6. **Use Relevant Visuals**: Ensure visuals are relevant to the content and enhance the message.
7. **Include Alt Text**: Use descriptive alt text for SEO and accessibility.
8. **Balance Text and Visuals**: Maintain a balance between

text and visuals for better readability.
9. **Use Visuals Consistently**: Ensure consistency in style and quality of visuals.
10. **Test Visual Impact**: A/B test different visuals to see which ones resonate best with your audience.

DAY 21: WRITING FOR DIFFERENT STAGES OF THE BUYER'S JOURNEY

Tailoring your copy for different stages of the buyer's journey can improve engagement and conversions. Here's how:

1. **Awareness Stage**: Focus on informative and educational content that addresses common problems or questions.
2. **Consideration Stage**: Provide detailed information about your product or service, including comparisons and case studies.
3. **Decision Stage**: Use persuasive copy that highlights benefits, testimonials, and CTAs to encourage purchase.
4. **Post-Purchase Stage**: Offer content that enhances the customer experience, such as user guides and thank you messages.
5. **Retention Stage**: Provide content that keeps customers engaged, such as newsletters, updates, and

loyalty programs.

6. **Use Different Formats**: Tailor content formats to each stage, such as blogs for awareness and detailed guides for consideration.
7. **Personalize Content**: Use personalization to make content more relevant to each stage.
8. **Track Behavior**: Use analytics to understand where your audience is in the buyer's journey and tailor content accordingly.
9. **Provide Value at Each Stage**: Ensure your content provides value at every stage of the journey.
10. **Align with Sales Funnel**: Ensure your content aligns with your overall sales funnel strategy.

DAY 22: THE IMPORTANCE OF A/B TESTING YOUR COPY

A/B testing helps you determine what works best for your audience. Here's how to do it effectively:

1. **Identify Goals**: Determine what you want to achieve with your A/B test, such as increased clicks or conversions.
2. **Choose Variables**: Decide which elements to test, such as headlines, CTAs, or images.
3. **Create Variations**: Develop two or more variations to test against each other.
4. **Split Your Audience**: Randomly split your audience to ensure unbiased results.
5. **Run the Test**: Conduct the test for a sufficient period to gather meaningful data.
6. **Analyze Results**: Compare the performance of each variation based on your goals.
7. **Implement Findings**: Use the winning variation to optimize your content.
8. **Test One Element at a Time**: Test one variable

at a time to isolate its impact.
9. **Use Tools**: Utilize A/B testing tools to simplify the process.
10. **Continuously Test**: Regularly conduct A/B tests to continuously improve your content.

DAY 23: COPYWRITING FOR E-COMMERCE WEBSITES

Effective copywriting can drive sales and conversions on e-commerce websites. Here's how to do it:

1. **Create Compelling Product Descriptions**: Highlight benefits, use sensory words, and be concise.
2. **Use Persuasive CTAs**: Include clear and compelling CTAs that guide visitors towards purchase.
3. **Incorporate Social Proof**: Use customer reviews, ratings, and testimonials.
4. **Highlight Unique Selling Points (USPs)**: Emphasize what makes your products unique.
5. **Provide Detailed Information**: Include all necessary details to help customers make informed decisions.
6. **Use High-Quality Images**: Complement descriptions with high-quality product images.
7. **Optimize for SEO**: Use relevant keywords in

product titles and descriptions.
8. **Simplify the Checkout Process**: Use clear and concise copy to guide users through the checkout process.
9. **Offer Guarantees**: Provide guarantees and return policies to build trust.
10. **Create Engaging Email Campaigns**: Use email campaigns to drive repeat purchases and build loyalty.

DAY 24: WRITING FOR MOBILE USERS

Writing for mobile users requires a different approach to ensure readability and engagement. Here's how to do it:

1. **Use Short Sentences and Paragraphs**: Keep sentences and paragraphs short for easy reading on small screens.
2. **Use Simple Language**: Avoid complex words and jargon.
3. **Use Clear Headings**: Use descriptive headings to break up content.
4. **Prioritize Important Information**: Place the most important information at the top.
5. **Use Bullet Points and Lists**: Use bullet points and lists to make content scannable.
6. **Optimize Images**: Use images that load quickly and are optimized for mobile.
7. **Use Responsive Design**: Ensure your website is responsive and mobile-friendly.
8. **Include Clear CTAs**: Use prominent and easy-to-click CTAs.

9. **Test on Mobile Devices**: Regularly test your content on different mobile devices.
10. **Simplify Navigation**: Ensure your mobile site is easy to navigate.

DAY 25: WRITING EFFECTIVE ABOUT US PAGES

Your About Us page is crucial for building trust and credibility. Here's how to write an effective one:

1. **Tell Your Story**: Share the story of your company, including its history and mission.
2. **Highlight Your Values**: Emphasize the values and principles that guide your company.
3. **Showcase Your Team**: Introduce your team with photos and brief bios.
4. **Use Authentic Language**: Write in a genuine and authentic tone.
5. **Include Visuals**: Use images and videos to make the page more engaging.
6. **Highlight Achievements**: Mention any awards, certifications, or notable achievements.
7. **Include Social Proof**: Add testimonials or quotes from satisfied customers.
8. **Provide Contact Information**: Make it easy for visitors to contact you.

9. **Keep It Updated**: Regularly update the page with new information.
10. **Include a CTA**: Encourage visitors to take the next step, such as signing up for a newsletter or contacting you.

DAY 26: CREATING HIGH-CONVERTING CTAS

A strong call-to-action (CTA) can significantly impact your conversions. Here's how to create high-converting CTAs:

1. **Use Action-Oriented Language**: Use verbs that encourage action, such as "Buy Now" or "Sign Up."
2. **Make It Stand Out**: Use contrasting colors and bold fonts to make your CTA button stand out.
3. **Keep It Short**: Be concise and to the point.
4. **Highlight Benefits**: Emphasize what the user will gain by taking action.
5. **Create Urgency**: Use words that create a sense of urgency, such as "Limited Time Offer" or "Only a Few Left."
6. **Place Strategically**: Position your CTAs where they are easily noticeable.
7. **Use First-Person Language**: Phrasing like "Get My Free Trial" can be more engaging.
8. **A/B Test CTAs**: Test different versions to see which

performs best.
9. **Ensure Mobile Friendliness**: Make sure your CTAs are easy to click on mobile devices.
10. **Align with Your Goal**: Ensure your CTA aligns with your overall marketing goal.

DAY 27: THE POWER OF HEADLINES

A compelling headline can draw readers in and set the tone for your content. Here's how to craft powerful headlines:

1. **Be Clear and Specific**: Clearly convey what the content is about.
2. **Use Numbers**: Numbers can make your headline more compelling and specific, such as "10 Tips for…"
3. **Address the Reader**: Use words like "you" to make it more personal.
4. **Create Curiosity**: Write headlines that pique curiosity and encourage clicks.
5. **Include Keywords**: Use relevant keywords for SEO.
6. **Keep It Short**: Aim for headlines that are short and to the point.
7. **Use Power Words**: Words like "amazing," "ultimate," and "essential" can make your headline more compelling.
8. **Test Different Headlines**: A/B test different headlines to see which performs best.
9. **Align with Content**: Ensure your headline accurately

reflects the content.
10. **Use Questions**: Headlines that ask a question can engage readers more effectively.

DAY 28: CREATING CONTENT THAT CONVERTS

Creating content that converts requires a strategic approach. Here's how to do it:

1. **Know Your Audience**: Understand the needs and preferences of your target audience.
2. **Provide Value**: Offer content that is valuable and relevant to your audience.
3. **Use Strong CTAs**: Include clear and compelling calls-to-action.
4. **Build Trust**: Use social proof, such as testimonials and reviews.
5. **Create Engaging Headlines**: Write headlines that grab attention and encourage clicks.
6. **Use Visuals**: Incorporate images, videos, and infographics to enhance your content.
7. **Optimize for SEO**: Use relevant keywords and follow SEO best practices.
8. **Make It Easy to Read**: Use headings, bullet points, and short paragraphs.

9. **Test and Optimize**: Continuously test and optimize your content for better performance.
10. **Track Conversions**: Use analytics to track the effectiveness of your content in driving conversions.

DAY 29: THE IMPACT OF USER-GENERATED CONTENT

User-generated content (UGC) can enhance your brand's credibility and engagement. Here's how to leverage it:

1. **Encourage Reviews**: Invite customers to leave reviews on your website and social media.
2. **Showcase Testimonials**: Highlight positive testimonials from satisfied customers.
3. **Feature Social Media Posts**: Share user-generated content from social media on your website.
4. **Create Contests and Campaigns**: Run contests that encourage users to create content.
5. **Use Hashtags**: Create branded hashtags for users to tag their content.
6. **Share Customer Stories**: Feature detailed customer stories or case studies.
7. **Offer Incentives**: Provide incentives for users to create and share content.
8. **Engage with UGC**: Respond to and engage with

user-generated content.
9. **Use UGC in Marketing**: Incorporate user-generated content in your marketing campaigns.
10. **Monitor and Moderate**: Regularly monitor and moderate user-generated content to maintain quality.

DAY 30: WRITING FOR DIFFERENT PLATFORMS

Different platforms require different approaches to copywriting. Here's how to tailor your writing:

1. **Social Media**: Use short, engaging posts with a clear CTA.
2. **Blog Posts**: Provide in-depth, valuable content with a conversational tone.
3. **Email**: Be concise and personal, with a strong subject line and CTA.
4. **Website Copy**: Focus on clarity, benefits, and SEO.
5. **Landing Pages**: Use persuasive, benefit-focused copy with a clear CTA.
6. **Product Descriptions**: Highlight features and benefits concisely.
7. **Ads**: Be brief and compelling, with a strong headline and CTA.
8. **Videos**: Write scripts that are engaging and to the point.

9. **Whitepapers**: Provide detailed, well-researched content.
10. **Newsletters**: Offer valuable information and updates with a personal touch.

DAY 31: CRAFTING CLEAR AND COMPELLING OFFERS

Clear and compelling offers can drive conversions and sales. Here's how to craft them:

1. **Highlight Benefits**: Emphasize the benefits of your offer.
2. **Use Clear Language**: Be clear and concise in your wording.
3. **Create Urgency**: Use time-limited offers to create urgency.
4. **Use Persuasive CTAs**: Include strong and clear CTAs.
5. **Provide Proof**: Use testimonials and case studies to support your offer.
6. **Offer Incentives**: Provide discounts, bonuses, or free trials.
7. **Be Transparent**: Clearly state any terms and conditions.
8. **Use Engaging Visuals**: Incorporate visuals that enhance the appeal of your offer.

9. **Personalize Offers**: Tailor offers to different segments of your audience.
10. **Test Different Offers**: Test various offers to see which performs best.

DAY 32: WRITING FOR B2B AUDIENCES

Writing for B2B audiences requires a different approach than B2C. Here's how to do it effectively:

1. **Focus on Value**: Highlight the value and benefits of your product or service.
2. **Use Professional Language**: Use a more formal and professional tone.
3. **Provide Detailed Information**: Offer in-depth information and data.
4. **Use Case Studies**: Provide case studies that demonstrate success.
5. **Address Pain Points**: Focus on addressing the specific pain points of businesses.
6. **Highlight ROI**: Emphasize the return on investment.
7. **Include Testimonials**: Use testimonials from other businesses.
8. **Use Clear CTAs**: Include clear and compelling CTAs.
9. **Personalize Content**: Tailor content to different roles and industries.

10. **Provide Resources**: Offer valuable resources, such as whitepapers and webinars.

DAY 33: THE ROLE OF EMOTIONS IN COPYWRITING

Emotions can significantly impact the effectiveness of your copy. Here's how to leverage them:

1. **Understand Your Audience**: Know what emotions resonate with your audience.
2. **Use Storytelling**: Incorporate storytelling to evoke emotions.
3. **Use Descriptive Language**: Use vivid and descriptive language.
4. **Highlight Benefits**: Emphasize how your product or service can positively impact your audience.
5. **Use Social Proof**: Testimonials and reviews can evoke trust and credibility.
6. **Create Urgency**: Use language that creates a sense of urgency.
7. **Be Authentic**: Ensure your emotions come across as genuine.
8. **Use Visuals**: Incorporate images and videos that

evoke emotions.
9. **Focus on the Positive**: Highlight positive outcomes and benefits.
10. **Test Emotional Impact**: Test different emotional appeals to see which resonates best.

DAY 34: WRITING FOR SEO

Writing for SEO involves optimizing your content to rank higher in search engine results. Here's how to do it:

1. **Use Keywords Strategically**: Incorporate relevant keywords naturally throughout your content.
2. **Optimize Headlines**: Use keywords in your headlines and make them compelling.
3. **Write Meta Descriptions**: Craft concise and keyword-rich meta descriptions.
4. **Use Alt Text for Images**: Include descriptive alt text for all images.
5. **Create Quality Content**: Focus on providing valuable and high-quality content.
6. **Use Internal and External Links**: Include links to other relevant pages and external sources.
7. **Optimize for Mobile**: Ensure your content is mobile-friendly.
8. **Use Clear and Descriptive URLs**: Create URLs that include relevant keywords.
9. **Update Content Regularly**: Keep your content up-to-

date and relevant.
10. **Monitor SEO Performance**: Use tools to track your SEO performance and make adjustments as needed.

DAY 35: WRITING EFFECTIVE BLOG POSTS

Blog posts can drive traffic and engagement. Here's how to write effective blog posts:

1. **Choose a Relevant Topic**: Select topics that are relevant to your audience.
2. **Create Compelling Headlines**: Use headlines that grab attention and include keywords.
3. **Provide Value**: Offer valuable and informative content.
4. **Use Clear Structure**: Use headings, subheadings, and bullet points to structure your content.
5. **Include Visuals**: Use images, videos, and infographics to enhance your post.
6. **Use Internal Links**: Link to other relevant posts on your blog.
7. **Optimize for SEO**: Use relevant keywords and optimize for search engines.
8. **Include a CTA**: Encourage readers to take action, such as subscribing or commenting.

9. **Promote Your Posts**: Share your blog posts on social media and other channels.
10. **Engage with Readers**: Respond to comments and engage with your audience.

DAY 36: THE IMPORTANCE OF PROOFREADING AND EDITING

Proofreading and editing are crucial for ensuring your copy is clear and error-free. Here's how to do it:

1. **Take a Break**: Step away from your writing before proofreading to see it with fresh eyes.
2. **Read Aloud**: Read your copy aloud to catch errors and awkward phrasing.
3. **Use Tools**: Use grammar and spell-check tools to identify errors.
4. **Check for Clarity**: Ensure your copy is clear and easy to understand.
5. **Look for Consistency**: Check for consistency in tone, style, and formatting.
6. **Check for Accuracy**: Verify all facts, figures, and references.
7. **Get a Second Opinion**: Have someone else review your copy.

8. **Focus on One Thing at a Time**: Check for different types of errors separately.
9. **Review Headings and CTAs**: Ensure headings and CTAs are clear and compelling.
10. **Edit Ruthlessly**: Be willing to cut unnecessary words and content.

DAY 37: COPYWRITING TRENDS TO WATCH

Staying updated with the latest copywriting trends can help you stay ahead. Here are some trends to watch:

1. **Conversational Copy**: Using a conversational tone to engage readers.
2. **Personalization**: Tailoring content to individual preferences and behaviors.
3. **Storytelling**: Using storytelling to create emotional connections.
4. **Interactive Content**: Incorporating interactive elements, such as quizzes and polls.
5. **Voice Search Optimization**: Optimizing for voice search queries.
6. **AI and Automation**: Using AI tools to enhance copywriting.
7. **Inclusive Language**: Using inclusive and diverse language.
8. **Visual Storytelling**: Combining visuals and copy to tell a story.

9. **Short-Form Content**: Creating short, impactful content.
10. **Sustainability Messaging**: Highlighting sustainable and ethical practices.

DAY 38: WRITING FOR DIFFERENT INDUSTRIES

Different industries require tailored approaches to copywriting. Here's how to write for various industries:

1. **Technology**: Use clear, concise language to explain complex concepts and focus on innovation and benefits.
2. **Healthcare**: Emphasize empathy, accuracy, and trustworthiness while simplifying medical jargon.
3. **Finance**: Focus on security, trust, and clear explanations of financial terms and benefits.
4. **Retail**: Highlight product benefits, customer testimonials, and create a sense of urgency.
5. **Real Estate**: Use descriptive language to paint a picture and emphasize the lifestyle benefits of properties.
6. **Travel**: Use vivid imagery and storytelling to evoke emotions and inspire wanderlust.
7. **Education**: Focus on outcomes, credibility, and

the transformative power of education.
8. **Nonprofits**: Emphasize the mission, impact, and ways to get involved or contribute.
9. **B2B Services**: Highlight ROI, case studies, and detailed benefits tailored to business needs.
10. **Automotive**: Focus on features, performance, and the driving experience, using high-quality visuals.

DAY 39: EFFECTIVE COPYWRITING FOR SOCIAL MEDIA ADS

Social media ads require concise, impactful copy. Here's how to create effective social media ads:

1. **Use Attention-Grabbing Headlines**: Start with a headline that grabs attention immediately.
2. **Be Concise**: Keep your copy short and to the point.
3. **Use Strong Visuals**: Pair your copy with eye-catching visuals.
4. **Include a Clear CTA**: Make your call-to-action clear and compelling.
5. **Highlight Benefits**: Focus on the benefits your audience will gain.
6. **Use Emojis**: Incorporate emojis to make your ad more engaging and relatable.
7. **Leverage Social Proof**: Include testimonials or user-generated content.
8. **Test Different Variations**: A/B test different versions of your ads.

9. **Tailor to the Platform**: Adjust your copy to fit the tone and format of each social media platform.
10. **Monitor Performance**: Track the performance of your ads and make necessary adjustments.

DAY 40: WRITING PERSUASIVE PRODUCT DESCRIPTIONS

Product descriptions need to be both informative and persuasive. Here's how to write them:

1. **Highlight Key Features**: Clearly outline the main features of the product.
2. **Focus on Benefits**: Emphasize the benefits and how the product solves a problem or improves life.
3. **Use Sensory Words**: Use descriptive words that appeal to the senses.
4. **Tell a Story**: Create a narrative around the product's use or origin.
5. **Incorporate Keywords**: Use relevant keywords for SEO purposes.
6. **Be Concise**: Keep the description short and to the point.
7. **Use Bullet Points**: Break up text with bullet

points for easy reading.
8. **Include Social Proof**: Add customer reviews and testimonials.
9. **Use High-Quality Images**: Pair the description with high-quality images or videos.
10. **Create Urgency**: Use phrases that create a sense of urgency or scarcity.

DAY 41: ENHANCING COPY WITH INTERACTIVE ELEMENTS

Interactive elements can make your copy more engaging. Here's how to use them:

1. **Quizzes**: Create quizzes that are relevant to your content and audience.
2. **Polls**: Use polls to engage your audience and gather feedback.
3. **Interactive Infographics**: Use interactive infographics to present data dynamically.
4. **Calculators**: Offer calculators that help users solve specific problems.
5. **Interactive Videos**: Use videos that allow viewers to make choices or interact.
6. **Surveys**: Incorporate surveys to collect insights and opinions.
7. **Games**: Create simple games that tie into your brand or message.

8. **Interactive Maps**: Use maps that users can interact with to explore information.
9. **Chatbots**: Implement chatbots to provide information and engage users.
10. **Interactive Content on Social Media**: Use interactive posts and stories on social media platforms.

DAY 42: CRAFTING COMPELLING BRAND STORIES

A strong brand story can differentiate your brand and create an emotional connection. Here's how to craft one:

1. **Define Your Mission**: Clearly articulate your brand's mission and purpose.
2. **Highlight Your History**: Share the history and origins of your brand.
3. **Showcase Your Values**: Emphasize the core values that guide your brand.
4. **Introduce Key Characters**: Introduce the people behind your brand, such as founders and employees.
5. **Use Real Stories**: Share real customer stories and experiences.
6. **Focus on Transformation**: Highlight how your brand brings about positive change.
7. **Be Authentic**: Ensure your story is genuine and true to your brand.
8. **Use Visuals**: Incorporate images and videos to

bring your story to life.
9. **Keep It Consistent**: Maintain consistency in your story across all platforms and materials.
10. **Engage Emotionally**: Connect with your audience on an emotional level.

DAY 43: WRITING FOR VIDEO SCRIPTS

Video scripts require a different approach to writing. Here's how to write effective video scripts:

1. **Start with a Strong Hook**: Capture the viewer's attention in the first few seconds.
2. **Keep It Concise**: Be concise and get to the point quickly.
3. **Use a Conversational Tone**: Write in a conversational tone to engage viewers.
4. **Include Visual and Audio Cues**: Indicate where visuals and audio elements will appear.
5. **Focus on Benefits**: Emphasize the benefits of your product or service.
6. **Use Storytelling**: Incorporate storytelling elements to make the video more engaging.
7. **Include a Clear CTA**: End with a clear and compelling call-to-action.
8. **Write for the Audience**: Tailor your script to the interests and needs of your audience.
9. **Use Simple Language**: Avoid jargon and complex words.

10. **Edit and Revise**: Review and revise your script to ensure clarity and impact.

DAY 44: WRITING ENGAGING EMAIL SUBJECT LINES

The subject line is crucial for the success of your email campaigns. Here's how to write engaging subject lines:

1. **Be Concise**: Keep your subject lines short and to the point.
2. **Create Urgency**: Use words that create a sense of urgency.
3. **Personalize**: Use the recipient's name or other personalized elements.
4. **Use Numbers**: Numbers can make your subject line more compelling.
5. **Ask Questions**: Questions can pique curiosity.
6. **Use Emojis**: Emojis can make your subject line stand out.
7. **Be Clear**: Clearly convey the main message or benefit.
8. **Create Intrigue**: Use words that create intrigue and encourage opens.
9. **Test Different Variations**: A/B test different

subject lines.
10. **Avoid Spam Triggers**: Avoid words and phrases that could trigger spam filters.

DAY 45: THE ROLE OF CONSISTENCY IN COPYWRITING

Consistency is key to building a strong brand. Here's how to maintain consistency in your copywriting:

1. **Develop a Style Guide**: Create a style guide that outlines your brand's tone, voice, and style.
2. **Use Consistent Tone and Voice**: Maintain a consistent tone and voice across all content.
3. **Align with Brand Values**: Ensure all content aligns with your brand's values and mission.
4. **Use Templates**: Use templates for recurring content types.
5. **Regular Training**: Train your team regularly on your brand's style and guidelines.
6. **Review and Edit**: Regularly review and edit content to ensure consistency.
7. **Use Consistent Visuals**: Pair your copy with consistent visual elements.
8. **Monitor All Channels**: Ensure consistency across all channels, including social media,

email, and website.
9. **Gather Feedback**: Regularly gather feedback to ensure your content remains consistent.
10. **Adapt to Changes**: Update your style guide as your brand evolves.

DAY 46: LEVERAGING USER FEEDBACK IN COPYWRITING

User feedback can provide valuable insights for your copywriting. Here's how to leverage it:

1. **Collect Feedback Regularly**: Use surveys, reviews, and direct feedback to gather insights.
2. **Identify Common Themes**: Look for common themes and issues in the feedback.
3. **Address Pain Points**: Use feedback to address common pain points in your copy.
4. **Highlight Positive Feedback**: Incorporate positive feedback and testimonials into your copy.
5. **Use Language from Feedback**: Use the language and terminology your users use.
6. **Test Changes**: Use feedback to make changes and test their impact.
7. **Showcase User Stories**: Share user stories and case studies.
8. **Engage with Feedback**: Respond to feedback

and show that you value it.
9. **Make Continuous Improvements**: Use feedback to make continuous improvements to your copy.
10. **Share Feedback Internally**: Share user feedback with your team to keep everyone informed.

DAY 47: WRITING FOR GLOBAL AUDIENCES

Writing for a global audience requires cultural sensitivity and adaptability. Here's how to do it:

1. **Use Simple Language**: Avoid idioms and complex language that may not translate well.
2. **Be Culturally Sensitive**: Be aware of cultural differences and avoid content that could be offensive.
3. **Localize Content**: Adapt your content to the local culture and language.
4. **Use Clear Examples**: Use examples that are universally understood.
5. **Avoid Jargon**: Avoid industry-specific jargon that may not be understood globally.
6. **Focus on Universal Themes**: Focus on themes and messages that resonate universally.
7. **Use Professional Translation Services**: Use professional services for accurate translation.
8. **Test with Local Audiences**: Test your

content with local audiences to ensure it resonates.
9. **Be Aware of Time Zones**: Consider different time zones when scheduling content.
10. **Respect Local Regulations**: Be aware of and comply with local regulations and standards.

DAY 48: WRITING FOR DIFFERENT GENERATIONS

Different generations respond to different types of content. Here's how to tailor your copy:

1. **Baby Boomers**: Use formal language and emphasize reliability and trust.
2. **Generation X**: Focus on practicality and value, using straightforward language.
3. **Millennials**: Use a casual tone, highlight experiences, and emphasize social proof.
4. **Generation Z**: Use short, visual content, and focus on authenticity and inclusivity.
5. **Adapt Tone and Style**: Adjust your tone and style to match the preferences of each generation.
6. **Use Appropriate Platforms**: Use the platforms that each generation prefers.
7. **Highlight Different Benefits**: Emphasize benefits that resonate with each generation.
8. **Incorporate Visuals**: Use visuals that appeal to

different age groups.
9. **Engage with Trends**: Stay updated with trends that are popular among different generations.
10. **Gather Feedback**: Collect feedback from different age groups to refine your approach.

DAY 49: WRITING COMPELLING CASE STUDIES

Case studies can showcase the effectiveness of your product or service. Here's how to write compelling case studies:

1. **Choose a Relevant Subject**: Select a subject that is relevant to your target audience.
2. **Provide Background Information**: Give context and background information about the subject.
3. **Describe the Problem**: Clearly outline the problem or challenge faced by the subject.
4. **Highlight the Solution**: Explain how your product or service provided a solution.
5. **Use Data and Metrics**: Include data and metrics to support your claims.
6. **Incorporate Quotes**: Use quotes from the subject to add authenticity.
7. **Showcase Results**: Highlight the results and benefits achieved.
8. **Use Visuals**: Include images, charts, and graphs to

illustrate the case study.
9. **Keep It Concise**: Be concise and focus on the key points.
10. **Include a CTA**: End with a clear call-to-action.

DAY 50: THE POWER OF STORYTELLING IN COPYWRITING

Storytelling can make your copy more engaging and memorable. Here's how to use storytelling in copywriting:

1. **Start with a Hook**: Capture attention with an intriguing opening.
2. **Introduce Characters**: Introduce relatable characters in your story.
3. **Create a Conflict**: Present a problem or challenge that needs to be solved.
4. **Show the Journey**: Describe the journey and actions taken to solve the problem.
5. **Highlight the Resolution**: Show how the problem was resolved.
6. **Use Emotional Appeal**: Evoke emotions through your story.
7. **Be Authentic**: Ensure your story is genuine and authentic.
8. **Use Vivid Language**: Use descriptive language to paint a picture.

9. **Keep It Simple**: Keep your story simple and focused.
10. **Align with Your Message**: Ensure your story aligns with your overall message.

DAY 51: WRITING FOR VOICE SEARCH

Voice search is becoming increasingly popular. Here's how to write for voice search:

1. **Use Natural Language**: Write in a conversational tone that mimics natural speech.
2. **Answer Questions**: Focus on answering common questions your audience may have.
3. **Use Long-Tail Keywords**: Incorporate long-tail keywords that reflect how people speak.
4. **Optimize for Featured Snippets**: Structure your content to be easily picked up as featured snippets.
5. **Focus on Local SEO**: Optimize for local searches if applicable.
6. **Provide Clear Answers**: Offer clear and concise answers to questions.
7. **Use Structured Data**: Implement structured data to help search engines understand your content.
8. **Keep It Simple**: Avoid complex sentences and jargon.

9. **Write for Mobile**: Ensure your content is mobile-friendly.
10. **Test with Voice Assistants**: Test your content using voice assistants to see how it performs.

DAY 52: WRITING FOR EMAIL MARKETING

Effective email marketing requires engaging and persuasive copy. Here's how to write for email marketing:

1. **Craft Compelling Subject Lines**: Use subject lines that grab attention and encourage opens.
2. **Use Personalization**: Personalize your emails with the recipient's name and other details.
3. **Be Concise**: Keep your email content short and to the point.
4. **Use a Clear CTA**: Include a clear and compelling call-to-action.
5. **Focus on Benefits**: Emphasize the benefits to the recipient.
6. **Use Visuals**: Incorporate images and videos to enhance your email.
7. **Segment Your Audience**: Tailor your emails to different segments of your audience.
8. **Test and Optimize**: Continuously test and optimize your emails for better performance.
9. **Include Social Proof**: Use testimonials and reviews to build credibility.

10. **Track Performance**: Monitor the performance of your emails and make adjustments as needed.

DAY 53: THE IMPORTANCE OF VISUAL COPYWRITING

Visual copywriting involves combining visuals and text to create engaging content. Here's how to do it:

1. **Use High-Quality Images**: Pair your copy with high-quality images that enhance your message.
2. **Incorporate Infographics**: Use infographics to present data and information visually.
3. **Use Video Content**: Create videos that combine visual and textual elements.
4. **Use Bold Typography**: Use bold and clear typography to highlight key points.
5. **Maintain Consistency**: Ensure visual and textual elements are consistent with your brand.
6. **Use Visual Storytelling**: Combine visuals and text to tell a compelling story.
7. **Optimize for Mobile**: Ensure your visual content is mobile-friendly.

8. **Use Color Strategically**: Use colors that align with your brand and enhance readability.
9. **Include Visual CTAs**: Use visually appealing call-to-action buttons.
10. **Test Different Formats**: Test various visual formats to see what works best.

DAY 54: WRITING FOR DIFFERENT CONTENT FORMATS

Different content formats require different approaches. Here's how to write for various formats:

1. **Blog Posts**: Provide in-depth information with a conversational tone and clear structure.
2. **Social Media Posts**: Use concise and engaging copy with a clear CTA.
3. **Whitepapers**: Offer detailed, well-researched content with a formal tone.
4. **Ebooks**: Provide comprehensive content organized into clear chapters.
5. **Newsletters**: Offer valuable information and updates with a personal touch.
6. **Press Releases**: Use a formal tone and focus on newsworthy information.
7. **Product Descriptions**: Highlight key features and benefits concisely.
8. **Landing Pages**: Use persuasive, benefit-focused copy with a clear CTA.

9. **Video Scripts**: Write engaging and concise scripts with visual and audio cues.
10. **Email Campaigns**: Be concise, personal, and include a strong subject line and CTA.

DAY 55: WRITING ENGAGING WEBINAR CONTENT

Webinars can be a powerful tool for engagement and education. Here's how to write engaging webinar content:

1. **Define Your Goals**: Clearly outline the goals and objectives of your webinar.
2. **Know Your Audience**: Understand the needs and interests of your audience.
3. **Create an Outline**: Develop a detailed outline to structure your webinar.
4. **Use Engaging Visuals**: Incorporate visuals, such as slides and videos, to enhance your presentation.
5. **Write a Strong Opening**: Start with an engaging opening to capture attention.
6. **Use Stories and Examples**: Use stories and real-life examples to illustrate your points.
7. **Include Interactive Elements**: Incorporate polls, quizzes, and Q&A sessions.
8. **Keep It Concise**: Be concise and avoid overwhelming

your audience with too much information.
9. **End with a CTA**: Conclude with a clear call-to-action.
10. **Practice and Rehearse**: Practice your webinar to ensure smooth delivery.

DAY 56: WRITING FOR PRODUCT LAUNCHES

Product launches require strategic and persuasive copy. Here's how to write for product launches:

1. **Create Anticipation**: Use teasers and previews to build anticipation.
2. **Highlight Unique Features**: Emphasize what makes your product unique.
3. **Focus on Benefits**: Clearly communicate the benefits to the user.
4. **Use Social Proof**: Incorporate testimonials and early reviews.
5. **Create Urgency**: Use limited-time offers to create a sense of urgency.
6. **Use Compelling Visuals**: Pair your copy with high-quality images and videos.
7. **Provide Detailed Information**: Offer detailed information about the product.
8. **Include a Clear CTA**: Use a clear and compelling call-to-action.
9. **Leverage Multiple Channels**: Promote your launch across various channels.

10. **Monitor and Adjust**: Track the performance of your launch and make necessary adjustments.

DAY 57: WRITING FOR NONPROFIT ORGANIZATIONS

Nonprofit organizations require a unique approach to copywriting. Here's how to do it effectively:
1. **Highlight the Mission**: Clearly articulate the mission and goals of the organization.
2. **Use Emotional Appeal**: Use emotional storytelling to connect with your audience.
3. **Showcase Impact**: Highlight the impact of the organization's work.
4. **Use Testimonials**: Incorporate testimonials from beneficiaries and supporters.
5. **Provide Clear CTAs**: Use clear calls-to-action for donations, volunteering, and other support.
6. **Be Transparent**: Ensure transparency about how funds and resources are used.
7. **Use Compelling Visuals**: Pair your copy with powerful images and videos.
8. **Engage with Supporters**: Engage with your

audience through newsletters, social media, and events.
9. **Share Success Stories**: Share stories of success and positive outcomes.
10. **Express Gratitude**: Show appreciation to donors and supporters regularly.

DAY 58: WRITING FOR EVENT PROMOTION

Effective event promotion requires engaging and informative copy. Here's how to do it:

1. **Create a Strong Hook**: Start with a compelling hook to capture interest.
2. **Provide Key Details**: Include essential details such as date, time, location, and agenda.
3. **Highlight Benefits**: Emphasize the benefits of attending the event.
4. **Use Social Proof**: Include testimonials from past attendees.
5. **Create Urgency**: Use limited-time offers or early bird discounts to create urgency.
6. **Use Visuals**: Incorporate images and videos to make your promotion more engaging.
7. **Include a Clear CTA**: Use a clear call-to-action for registration or ticket purchase.
8. **Leverage Multiple Channels**: Promote the event across various channels.
9. **Engage with Attendees**: Engage with potential attendees through social media and email.

10. **Follow Up**: Follow up with attendees after the event for feedback and future engagement.

DAY 59: WRITING FOR ONLINE COURSES

Online courses require clear and engaging content. Here's how to write for online courses:

1. **Define Learning Objectives**: Clearly outline the learning objectives for each module.
2. **Use Clear Structure**: Use headings, subheadings, and bullet points to structure your content.
3. **Incorporate Visuals**: Use images, videos, and infographics to enhance learning.
4. **Use Interactive Elements**: Incorporate quizzes, assignments, and interactive activities.
5. **Be Concise**: Keep your content concise and to the point.
6. **Use Real-Life Examples**: Use real-life examples to illustrate concepts.
7. **Provide Additional Resources**: Include links to additional resources and readings.
8. **Encourage Engagement**: Encourage discussion and interaction among participants.

9. **Use Clear Instructions**: Provide clear instructions for assignments and activities.
10. **Monitor Progress**: Track participant progress and provide feedback.

DAY 60: WRITING FOR CROWDFUNDING CAMPAIGNS

Crowdfunding campaigns require persuasive and compelling copy. Here's how to write for crowdfunding:

1. **Tell a Compelling Story**: Use storytelling to explain the purpose of your campaign.
2. **Highlight the Problem**: Clearly outline the problem or need.
3. **Showcase the Solution**: Explain how your campaign provides a solution.
4. **Use Emotional Appeal**: Use emotional language to connect with potential backers.
5. **Provide Clear Details**: Include details about how funds will be used.
6. **Use Visuals**: Incorporate images and videos to make your campaign more engaging.
7. **Include Rewards**: Highlight the rewards for different levels of support.
8. **Create Urgency**: Use limited-time offers or milestones to create urgency.

9. **Engage with Backers**: Engage with backers through updates and communication.
10. **Show Gratitude**: Thank your backers and show appreciation for their support.

DAY 61: WRITING FOR PODCASTS

Podcast scripts need to be engaging and conversational. Here's how to write for podcasts:

1. **Start with a Strong Opening**: Capture attention with an interesting opening.
2. **Use a Conversational Tone**: Write in a conversational tone to engage listeners.
3. **Structure Your Content**: Use a clear structure with an introduction, body, and conclusion.
4. **Include Stories and Examples**: Use stories and examples to illustrate your points.
5. **Be Concise**: Keep your script concise and avoid unnecessary details.
6. **Use Questions**: Incorporate questions to engage your audience.
7. **Include a CTA**: End with a clear call-to-action.
8. **Practice and Rehearse**: Practice your script to ensure smooth delivery.
9. **Use Clear Language**: Avoid jargon and complex language.
10. **Edit and Revise**: Review and revise your script

for clarity and impact.

DAY 62: WRITING FOR VIDEO MARKETING

Video marketing requires engaging and persuasive scripts. Here's how to write for video marketing:

1. **Start with a Hook**: Capture attention in the first few seconds.
2. **Be Concise**: Keep your script short and to the point.
3. **Use a Conversational Tone**: Write in a conversational tone to engage viewers.
4. **Include Visual Cues**: Indicate where visuals and audio elements will appear.
5. **Focus on Benefits**: Emphasize the benefits of your product or service.
6. **Use Storytelling**: Incorporate storytelling elements to make the video more engaging.
7. **Include a Clear CTA**: End with a clear call-to-action.
8. **Write for the Audience**: Tailor your script to the interests and needs of your audience.
9. **Use Simple Language**: Avoid jargon and complex words.

10. **Edit and Revise**: Review and revise your script to ensure clarity and impact.

DAY 63: WRITING FOR PRINT ADVERTISING

Print advertising requires concise and impactful copy. Here's how to write for print advertising:

1. **Use a Strong Headline**: Start with a headline that grabs attention.
2. **Be Concise**: Keep your copy short and to the point.
3. **Highlight Benefits**: Focus on the benefits to the reader.
4. **Use Visuals**: Pair your copy with compelling visuals.
5. **Include a CTA**: Use a clear and compelling call-to-action.
6. **Use Bullet Points**: Break up text with bullet points for easy reading.
7. **Be Persuasive**: Use persuasive language to encourage action.
8. **Focus on One Message**: Focus on one main message to avoid confusion.
9. **Use White Space**: Use white space to make your ad more readable.

10. **Test Different Versions**: Test different versions of your ad to see what works best.

DAY 64: WRITING FOR INFLUENCER MARKETING

Influencer marketing involves collaborating with influencers to promote your brand. Here's how to write for influencer marketing:

1. **Choose the Right Influencers**: Select influencers who align with your brand values and audience.
2. **Provide Clear Guidelines**: Provide clear guidelines and expectations for the collaboration.
3. **Allow Creative Freedom**: Allow influencers creative freedom to maintain authenticity.
4. **Use Authentic Language**: Encourage influencers to use authentic and natural language.
5. **Highlight Key Messages**: Ensure key messages and benefits are clearly communicated.
6. **Incorporate Visuals**: Use visuals that align with the influencer's style and audience.
7. **Include a CTA**: Use a clear call-to-action in the influencer's content.
8. **Track Performance**: Monitor the performance of the

influencer's content.
9. **Engage with the Audience**: Engage with the influencer's audience through comments and interactions.
10. **Show Appreciation**: Show appreciation to the influencer and their audience.

DAY 65: WRITING FOR CRISIS COMMUNICATION

Crisis communication requires careful and thoughtful copywriting. Here's how to write for crisis communication:

1. **Be Transparent**: Be honest and transparent about the situation.
2. **Use Clear Language**: Use clear and straightforward language.
3. **Acknowledge the Issue**: Acknowledge the issue and take responsibility if necessary.
4. **Provide Reassurance**: Reassure your audience that the issue is being addressed.
5. **Offer Solutions**: Provide solutions or steps being taken to resolve the issue.
6. **Use Empathy**: Show empathy and understanding towards those affected.
7. **Keep It Concise**: Be concise and avoid unnecessary details.
8. **Update Regularly**: Provide regular updates on the

situation.
9. **Use Multiple Channels**: Communicate through multiple channels to reach a wider audience.
10. **Prepare in Advance**: Have a crisis communication plan in place before a crisis occurs.

DAY 66: WRITING FOR LANDING PAGES

Landing pages require persuasive and action-oriented copy. Here's how to write for landing pages:

1. **Use a Strong Headline**: Start with a compelling headline that grabs attention.
2. **Highlight Benefits**: Focus on the benefits to the visitor.
3. **Use Clear CTAs**: Include clear and compelling calls-to-action.
4. **Use Bullet Points**: Break up text with bullet points for easy reading.
5. **Include Social Proof**: Use testimonials and reviews to build credibility.
6. **Use Visuals**: Pair your copy with high-quality images and videos.
7. **Keep It Concise**: Be concise and avoid unnecessary details.
8. **Optimize for SEO**: Use relevant keywords and optimize for search engines.
9. **Test Different Versions**: A/B test different versions of your landing page.

10. **Monitor Performance**: Track the performance of your landing page and make adjustments as needed.

DAY 67: WRITING FOR USER ONBOARDING

User onboarding requires clear and helpful copy. Here's how to write for user onboarding:

1. **Welcome the User**: Start with a warm and welcoming message.
2. **Provide Clear Instructions**: Offer clear and concise instructions.
3. **Use Visual Aids**: Incorporate images, videos, and diagrams to help explain steps.
4. **Highlight Key Features**: Emphasize the key features and benefits.
5. **Be Concise**: Keep your copy short and to the point.
6. **Use a Friendly Tone**: Use a friendly and approachable tone.
7. **Offer Support**: Provide links to support resources and contact information.
8. **Gather Feedback**: Ask for feedback to improve the onboarding process.
9. **Track Progress**: Monitor the user's progress and offer assistance if needed.

10. **Update Regularly**: Keep your onboarding content updated with any changes or new features.

DAY 68: WRITING FOR CUSTOMER RETENTION

Customer retention requires engaging and value-driven copy. Here's how to write for customer retention:

1. **Show Appreciation**: Regularly thank your customers and show appreciation.
2. **Offer Exclusive Benefits**: Provide exclusive benefits and rewards to loyal customers.
3. **Personalize Communication**: Personalize your communication to make customers feel valued.
4. **Provide Value**: Offer valuable content, tips, and resources.
5. **Engage on Multiple Channels**: Engage with customers through email, social media, and other channels.
6. **Use Customer Feedback**: Use customer feedback to improve your products and services.
7. **Highlight Success Stories**: Share success stories and testimonials from satisfied customers.
8. **Be Responsive**: Respond quickly to customer

inquiries and issues.
9. **Offer Regular Updates**: Keep customers informed about new features, updates, and news.
10. **Build a Community**: Create a community where customers can interact and share experiences.

DAY 69: WRITING FOR SURVEYS AND FEEDBACK FORMS

Surveys and feedback forms require clear and concise copy. Here's how to write for surveys and feedback forms:

1. **Be Clear and Specific**: Use clear and specific questions.
2. **Keep It Short**: Keep your survey or feedback form short and to the point.
3. **Use Simple Language**: Avoid jargon and complex language.
4. **Include a Mix of Question Types**: Use a mix of multiple-choice, rating scales, and open-ended questions.
5. **Be Neutral**: Avoid leading questions that can bias responses.
6. **Provide Context**: Offer context or examples if needed.
7. **Use a Friendly Tone**: Use a friendly and approachable tone.
8. **Include a CTA**: Encourage respondents to

complete the survey with a clear CTA.
9. **Offer an Incentive**: Provide an incentive for completing the survey.
10. **Test Your Survey**: Test your survey with a small group before distributing it widely.

DAY 70: WRITING FOR SEO

SEO copywriting requires a strategic approach to improve search engine rankings. Here's how to write for SEO:

1. **Use Relevant Keywords**: Research and use relevant keywords throughout your content.
2. **Optimize Headings**: Use keywords in your headings and subheadings.
3. **Write Compelling Meta Descriptions**: Write engaging meta descriptions that include keywords.
4. **Use Alt Text for Images**: Include keywords in the alt text of images.
5. **Create High-Quality Content**: Focus on creating valuable and high-quality content.
6. **Use Internal Links**: Link to other relevant pages on your website.
7. **Optimize for Mobile**: Ensure your content is mobile-friendly.
8. **Use a Clear URL Structure**: Use a clear and descriptive URL structure.
9. **Incorporate External Links**: Link to reputable

external sources.
10. **Monitor Performance**: Track the performance of your SEO efforts and make adjustments as needed.

DAY 71: WRITING FOR E-COMMERCE

E-commerce copywriting requires persuasive and informative copy. Here's how to write for e-commerce:

1. **Use Compelling Product Titles**: Write clear and compelling product titles.
2. **Highlight Key Features**: Emphasize the key features and benefits of the product.
3. **Use High-Quality Images**: Pair your copy with high-quality product images.
4. **Include Customer Reviews**: Use customer reviews and ratings to build trust.
5. **Use a Clear CTA**: Include a clear call-to-action for purchasing.
6. **Be Concise**: Keep your copy concise and to the point.
7. **Use Bullet Points**: Break up text with bullet points for easy reading.
8. **Optimize for SEO**: Use relevant keywords to optimize your product pages for search engines.
9. **Provide Detailed Descriptions**: Offer detailed product descriptions to inform potential buyers.

10. **Use Persuasive Language**: Use persuasive language to encourage purchases.

DAY 72: WRITING FOR SALES PAGES

Sales pages require persuasive and action-oriented copy. Here's how to write for sales pages:

1. **Use a Strong Headline**: Start with a compelling headline that grabs attention.
2. **Highlight Benefits**: Focus on the benefits to the visitor.
3. **Use Social Proof**: Include testimonials and reviews to build credibility.
4. **Use Visuals**: Pair your copy with high-quality images and videos.
5. **Include a Clear CTA**: Use a clear and compelling call-to-action.
6. **Be Concise**: Keep your copy concise and avoid unnecessary details.
7. **Use Persuasive Language**: Use persuasive language to encourage action.
8. **Create Urgency**: Use limited-time offers or scarcity to create urgency.
9. **Test Different Versions**: A/B test different versions of your sales page.

10. **Monitor Performance**: Track the performance of your sales page and make adjustments as needed.

DAY 73: WRITING FOR EDUCATIONAL CONTENT

Educational content requires clear and informative copy. Here's how to write for educational content:

1. **Define Learning Objectives**: Clearly outline the learning objectives for your content.
2. **Use Clear Structure**: Use headings, subheadings, and bullet points to structure your content.
3. **Incorporate Visuals**: Use images, videos, and infographics to enhance learning.
4. **Use Simple Language**: Avoid jargon and complex language.
5. **Provide Real-Life Examples**: Use real-life examples to illustrate concepts.
6. **Include Interactive Elements**: Incorporate quizzes, assignments, and interactive activities.
7. **Be Concise**: Keep your content concise and to the point.
8. **Provide Additional Resources**: Include links to additional resources and readings.

9. **Encourage Engagement**: Encourage discussion and interaction among participants.
10. **Update Regularly**: Keep your educational content updated with the latest information and best practices.

DAY 74: WRITING FOR HEALTHCARE

Healthcare copywriting requires accuracy and sensitivity. Here's how to write for healthcare:

1. **Use Clear and Simple Language**: Avoid jargon and use language that is easy to understand.
2. **Be Accurate**: Ensure all information is accurate and based on reputable sources.
3. **Use a Compassionate Tone**: Use a compassionate and empathetic tone.
4. **Provide Clear Instructions**: Offer clear and concise instructions for health-related actions.
5. **Highlight Benefits**: Emphasize the benefits of health services or products.
6. **Use Visual Aids**: Incorporate images, videos, and diagrams to help explain health concepts.
7. **Be Sensitive**: Be mindful of sensitive health issues and topics.
8. **Include Disclaimers**: Include necessary disclaimers and legal information.
9. **Use Testimonials**: Use testimonials and

reviews from patients or users.
10. **Encourage Action**: Include a clear call-to-action for appointments, consultations, or purchases.

DAY 75: WRITING FOR FINANCE

Finance copywriting requires clarity and trustworthiness. Here's how to write for finance:

1. **Use Clear and Simple Language**: Avoid jargon and use language that is easy to understand.
2. **Be Accurate**: Ensure all information is accurate and based on reputable sources.
3. **Use a Trustworthy Tone**: Use a tone that conveys trust and reliability.
4. **Provide Clear Instructions**: Offer clear and concise instructions for financial actions.
5. **Highlight Benefits**: Emphasize the benefits of financial services or products.
6. **Use Visual Aids**: Incorporate charts, graphs, and diagrams to help explain financial concepts.
7. **Include Disclaimers**: Include necessary disclaimers and legal information.
8. **Use Testimonials**: Use testimonials and reviews from clients or users.
9. **Encourage Action**: Include a clear call-to-action for consultations, sign-ups, or purchases.

10. **Be Transparent**: Be transparent about fees, risks, and other important information.

DAY 76: WRITING FOR TECHNOLOGY

Technology copywriting requires clarity and innovation. Here's how to write for technology:

1. **Use Clear and Simple Language**: Avoid jargon and use language that is easy to understand.
2. **Highlight Features and Benefits**: Emphasize the features and benefits of the technology.
3. **Use Visual Aids**: Incorporate images, videos, and diagrams to help explain technology concepts.
4. **Be Accurate**: Ensure all information is accurate and based on reputable sources.
5. **Use a Professional Tone**: Use a tone that conveys expertise and professionalism.
6. **Provide Clear Instructions**: Offer clear and concise instructions for using the technology.
7. **Use Testimonials**: Use testimonials and reviews from users.
8. **Encourage Action**: Include a clear call-to-action for demos, sign-ups, or purchases.
9. **Be Concise**: Keep your copy concise and to the

point.
10. **Update Regularly**: Keep your technology content updated with the latest information and advancements.

DAY 77: WRITING FOR TRAVEL

Travel copywriting requires evocative and inspiring copy. Here's how to write for travel:

1. **Use Descriptive Language**: Use vivid and descriptive language to paint a picture.
2. **Highlight Unique Experiences**: Emphasize unique experiences and destinations.
3. **Use Visuals**: Incorporate high-quality images and videos to showcase travel destinations.
4. **Include Personal Stories**: Use personal stories and testimonials to add authenticity.
5. **Provide Practical Information**: Offer practical information such as travel tips and itineraries.
6. **Use a Conversational Tone**: Use a friendly and conversational tone.
7. **Highlight Benefits**: Emphasize the benefits of the travel experience.
8. **Include a CTA**: Use a clear call-to-action for bookings or inquiries.
9. **Be Honest**: Be honest about what travelers can expect.

10. **Update Regularly**: Keep your travel content updated with the latest information and trends.

DAY 78: WRITING FOR LIFESTYLE

Lifestyle copywriting requires engaging and relatable content. Here's how to write for lifestyle:

1. **Use a Conversational Tone**: Write in a conversational and relatable tone.
2. **Highlight Benefits**: Focus on the benefits to the reader's lifestyle.
3. **Use Personal Stories**: Incorporate personal stories and testimonials.
4. **Be Concise**: Keep your copy short and to the point.
5. **Use Visuals**: Pair your copy with high-quality images and videos.
6. **Provide Practical Tips**: Offer practical tips and advice.
7. **Use a Friendly Tone**: Use a friendly and approachable tone.
8. **Encourage Engagement**: Encourage reader engagement through comments and interactions.
9. **Be Honest**: Be honest and authentic in your

content.

10. **Update Regularly**: Keep your lifestyle content updated with the latest trends and information.

DAY 79: WRITING FOR SPORTS

Sports copywriting requires energetic and engaging content. Here's how to write for sports:

1. **Use Dynamic Language**: Use energetic and dynamic language to convey excitement.
2. **Highlight Key Moments**: Emphasize key moments and achievements.
3. **Use Visuals**: Incorporate high-quality images and videos to capture the action.
4. **Include Personal Stories**: Use personal stories and testimonials from athletes.
5. **Be Concise**: Keep your copy concise and to the point.
6. **Use a Conversational Tone**: Write in a conversational and engaging tone.
7. **Highlight Benefits**: Emphasize the benefits of sports participation or products.
8. **Include a CTA**: Use a clear call-to-action for sign-ups or purchases.
9. **Be Honest**: Be honest and authentic in your content.

10. **Update Regularly**: Keep your sports content updated with the latest news and information.

DAY 80: WRITING FOR REAL ESTATE

Real estate copywriting requires persuasive and informative content. Here's how to write for real estate:

1. **Use Descriptive Language**: Use vivid and descriptive language to paint a picture of the property.
2. **Highlight Key Features**: Emphasize the key features and benefits of the property.
3. **Use High-Quality Images**: Pair your copy with high-quality images and videos of the property.
4. **Include Testimonials**: Use testimonials and reviews from past clients.
5. **Be Concise**: Keep your copy concise and to the point.
6. **Use a Professional Tone**: Write in a professional and trustworthy tone.
7. **Provide Practical Information**: Offer practical information such as pricing, location, and amenities.
8. **Use a Clear CTA**: Include a clear call-to-action for inquiries or viewings.

9. **Be Honest**: Be honest about the property's features and condition.
10. **Update Regularly**: Keep your real estate content updated with the latest listings and market trends.

DAY 81: WRITING FOR B2B

B2B copywriting requires informative and persuasive content. Here's how to write for B2B:

1. **Use a Professional Tone**: Write in a professional and authoritative tone.
2. **Highlight Benefits**: Emphasize the benefits to the business.
3. **Use Data and Statistics**: Incorporate data and statistics to support your claims.
4. **Include Case Studies**: Use case studies and testimonials from other businesses.
5. **Be Concise**: Keep your copy concise and to the point.
6. **Provide Clear Instructions**: Offer clear and concise instructions for next steps.
7. **Use Visuals**: Incorporate images, charts, and diagrams to enhance your content.
8. **Include a Clear CTA**: Use a clear call-to-action for inquiries or consultations.
9. **Be Honest**: Be honest and transparent in your content.

10. **Update Regularly**: Keep your B2B content updated with the latest information and best practices.

DAY 82: WRITING FOR B2C

B2C copywriting requires engaging and persuasive content. Here's how to write for B2C:

1. **Use a Conversational Tone**: Write in a conversational and relatable tone.
2. **Highlight Benefits**: Focus on the benefits to the consumer.
3. **Use Emotional Appeal**: Use emotional language to connect with your audience.
4. **Include Testimonials**: Use testimonials and reviews from customers.
5. **Be Concise**: Keep your copy concise and to the point.
6. **Use Visuals**: Pair your copy with high-quality images and videos.
7. **Include a Clear CTA**: Use a clear call-to-action for purchases or sign-ups.
8. **Use Persuasive Language**: Use persuasive language to encourage action.
9. **Be Honest**: Be honest and authentic in your content.

10. **Update Regularly**: Keep your B2C content updated with the latest trends and information.

DAY 83: WRITING FOR NONPROFITS

Nonprofit copywriting requires emotional and persuasive content. Here's how to write for nonprofits:

1. **Highlight the Mission**: Clearly articulate the mission and goals of the organization.
2. **Use Emotional Appeal**: Use emotional storytelling to connect with your audience.
3. **Showcase Impact**: Highlight the impact of the organization's work.
4. **Use Testimonials**: Incorporate testimonials from beneficiaries and supporters.
5. **Provide Clear CTAs**: Use clear calls-to-action for donations, volunteering, and other support.
6. **Be Transparent**: Ensure transparency about how funds and resources are used.
7. **Use Compelling Visuals**: Pair your copy with powerful images and videos.
8. **Engage with Supporters**: Engage with your audience through newsletters, social media, and events.

9. **Share Success Stories**: Share stories of success and positive outcomes.
10. **Express Gratitude**: Show appreciation to donors and supporters regularly.

DAY 84: WRITING FOR INTERNAL COMMUNICATIONS

Internal communications require clear and engaging copy. Here's how to write for internal communications:

1. **Use Clear and Simple Language**: Avoid jargon and use language that is easy to understand.
2. **Be Concise**: Keep your messages concise and to the point.
3. **Use a Friendly Tone**: Use a friendly and approachable tone.
4. **Highlight Key Messages**: Emphasize the key messages and takeaways.
5. **Use Visuals**: Incorporate images, charts, and diagrams to enhance your content.
6. **Encourage Feedback**: Encourage feedback and interaction from employees.
7. **Provide Clear Instructions**: Offer clear and concise instructions for any actions required.
8. **Be Consistent**: Maintain a consistent tone and style across all communications.

9. **Use Multiple Channels**: Communicate through multiple channels to reach all employees.
10. **Update Regularly**: Keep your internal communications updated with the latest information and news.

DAY 85: WRITING FOR ACADEMIC CONTENT

Academic content requires clear and scholarly copy. Here's how to write for academic content:

1. **Use Clear and Simple Language**: Avoid jargon and use language that is easy to understand.
2. **Be Accurate**: Ensure all information is accurate and based on reputable sources.
3. **Use a Scholarly Tone**: Write in a professional and scholarly tone.
4. **Provide Clear Structure**: Use headings, subheadings, and bullet points to structure your content.
5. **Incorporate Visuals**: Use images, charts, and diagrams to enhance your content.
6. **Use Citations**: Properly cite all sources and references.
7. **Be Concise**: Keep your content concise and to the point.
8. **Provide Additional Resources**: Include links to additional readings and resources.
9. **Encourage Engagement**: Encourage

discussion and interaction among readers.
10. **Update Regularly**: Keep your academic content updated with the latest research and information.

DAY 86: WRITING FOR LEGAL CONTENT

Legal content requires clarity and precision. Here's how to write for legal content:

1. **Use Clear and Simple Language**: Avoid jargon and use language that is easy to understand.
2. **Be Accurate**: Ensure all information is accurate and based on reputable sources.
3. **Use a Formal Tone**: Write in a professional and formal tone.
4. **Provide Clear Structure**: Use headings, subheadings, and bullet points to structure your content.
5. **Incorporate Visuals**: Use charts and diagrams to help explain legal concepts.
6. **Use Citations**: Properly cite all sources and references.
7. **Be Concise**: Keep your content concise and to the point.
8. **Provide Clear Instructions**: Offer clear and concise instructions for any legal actions required.

9. **Include Disclaimers**: Include necessary disclaimers and legal information.
10. **Update Regularly**: Keep your legal content updated with the latest laws and regulations.

DAY 87: WRITING FOR EVENT PROMOTION

Event promotion requires engaging and persuasive copy. Here's how to write for event promotion:

1. **Use a Compelling Headline**: Start with a headline that grabs attention.
2. **Highlight Key Details**: Include the date, time, location, and key features of the event.
3. **Use Persuasive Language**: Use persuasive language to encourage attendance.
4. **Use Visuals**: Pair your copy with high-quality images and videos.
5. **Include Testimonials**: Use testimonials and reviews from past attendees.
6. **Be Concise**: Keep your copy concise and to the point.
7. **Use a Clear CTA**: Include a clear call-to-action for registrations or ticket purchases.
8. **Engage on Multiple Channels**: Promote your event through email, social media, and other channels.
9. **Be Honest**: Be honest about what attendees can

expect.
10. **Update Regularly**: Keep your event promotion content updated with the latest information and details.

DAY 88: WRITING FOR PRESS RELEASES

Press releases require clear and newsworthy content. Here's how to write for press releases:

1. **Use a Strong Headline**: Start with a headline that grabs attention.
2. **Include Key Information**: Include the who, what, when, where, and why.
3. **Use a Professional Tone**: Write in a professional and formal tone.
4. **Be Concise**: Keep your press release concise and to the point.
5. **Include Quotes**: Use quotes from key individuals involved.
6. **Provide Contact Information**: Include contact information for further inquiries.
7. **Use Visuals**: Pair your copy with images or videos if applicable.
8. **Be Newsworthy**: Ensure your press release is newsworthy and relevant.
9. **Use a Clear Structure**: Use headings and bullet points to structure your content.

10. **Distribute Widely**: Distribute your press release to relevant media outlets and platforms.

DAY 89: WRITING FOR EMAIL NEWSLETTERS

Email newsletters require engaging and informative content. Here's how to write for email newsletters:

1. **Use a Compelling Subject Line**: Start with a subject line that grabs attention.
2. **Be Concise**: Keep your email content concise and to the point.
3. **Use a Friendly Tone**: Write in a friendly and approachable tone.
4. **Include Visuals**: Pair your copy with high-quality images and videos.
5. **Provide Value**: Offer valuable content, tips, and resources.
6. **Use a Clear CTA**: Include a clear call-to-action for further engagement.
7. **Personalize Content**: Personalize your content to make it more relevant to the reader.
8. **Encourage Interaction**: Encourage readers to interact and provide feedback.
9. **Be Consistent**: Maintain a consistent schedule for your newsletters.

10. **Track Performance**: Monitor the performance of your newsletters and make adjustments as needed.

DAY 90: WRITING FOR SOCIAL MEDIA

Social media copywriting requires engaging and shareable content. Here's how to write for social media:

1. **Use a Conversational Tone**: Write in a conversational and relatable tone.
2. **Be Concise**: Keep your posts short and to the point.
3. **Use Visuals**: Pair your copy with high-quality images, videos, and infographics.
4. **Encourage Engagement**: Encourage likes, comments, shares, and interactions.
5. **Use Hashtags**: Use relevant hashtags to increase visibility.
6. **Provide Value**: Offer valuable content, tips, and resources.
7. **Be Authentic**: Be honest and authentic in your content.
8. **Include a CTA**: Use a clear call-to-action for further engagement.
9. **Be Consistent**: Maintain a consistent posting schedule.

10. **Track Performance**: Monitor the performance of your posts and make adjustments as needed.

DAY 91: WRITING FOR BLOGS

Blog copywriting requires informative and engaging content. Here's how to write for blogs:

1. **Use a Compelling Title**: Start with a title that grabs attention.
2. **Be Concise**: Keep your content concise and to the point.
3. **Use a Friendly Tone**: Write in a friendly and conversational tone.
4. **Provide Value**: Offer valuable content, tips, and resources.
5. **Use Visuals**: Pair your copy with high-quality images, videos, and infographics.
6. **Encourage Interaction**: Encourage comments and interactions from readers.
7. **Optimize for SEO**: Use relevant keywords and optimize your content for search engines.
8. **Use a Clear Structure**: Use headings, subheadings, and bullet points to structure your content.
9. **Include Links**: Include internal and external

links to provide additional value.
10. **Update Regularly**: Keep your blog content updated with the latest information and trends.

DAY 92: WRITING FOR VIDEO SCRIPTS REVISITED

Video scripts require engaging and clear content. Here's how to write for video scripts:

1. **Use a Conversational Tone**: Write in a conversational and relatable tone.
2. **Be Concise**: Keep your script concise and to the point.
3. **Use Visuals**: Pair your script with high-quality visuals and animations.
4. **Provide Clear Instructions**: Offer clear and concise instructions for any actions required.
5. **Include a CTA**: Use a clear call-to-action for further engagement.
6. **Be Authentic**: Be honest and authentic in your script.
7. **Use a Clear Structure**: Use a clear structure to organize your content.
8. **Incorporate Humor**: Use humor if appropriate to engage your audience.

9. **Practice Timing**: Ensure your script is timed appropriately for the video length.
10. **Review and Revise**: Review and revise your script for clarity and impact.

DAY 93: WRITING FOR PODCASTS REVISITED

Podcast scripts require engaging and conversational content. Here's how to write for podcasts:

1. **Use a Conversational Tone**: Write in a conversational and relatable tone.
2. **Be Concise**: Keep your script concise and to the point.
3. **Provide Value**: Offer valuable content, tips, and resources.
4. **Use Visuals**: Incorporate sound effects and music to enhance your podcast.
5. **Include a CTA**: Use a clear call-to-action for further engagement.
6. **Be Authentic**: Be honest and authentic in your script.
7. **Use a Clear Structure**: Use a clear structure to organize your content.
8. **Incorporate Humor**: Use humor if appropriate to engage your audience.
9. **Practice Timing**: Ensure your script is timed appropriately for the podcast length.

10. **Review and Revise**: Review and revise your script for clarity and impact.

DAY 94: WRITING FOR WEBINARS

Webinar scripts require engaging and informative content. Here's how to write for webinars:

1. **Use a Conversational Tone**: Write in a conversational and relatable tone.
2. **Be Concise**: Keep your script concise and to the point.
3. **Provide Value**: Offer valuable content, tips, and resources.
4. **Use Visuals**: Pair your script with high-quality visuals and slides.
5. **Include a CTA**: Use a clear call-to-action for further engagement.
6. **Be Authentic**: Be honest and authentic in your script.
7. **Use a Clear Structure**: Use a clear structure to organize your content.
8. **Incorporate Humor**: Use humor if appropriate to engage your audience.
9. **Practice Timing**: Ensure your script is timed appropriately for the webinar length.

10. **Review and Revise**: Review and revise your script for clarity and impact.

DAY 95: WRITING FOR PRESENTATIONS

Presentation scripts require clear and engaging content. Here's how to write for presentations:

1. **Use a Conversational Tone**: Write in a conversational and relatable tone.
2. **Be Concise**: Keep your script concise and to the point.
3. **Provide Value**: Offer valuable content, tips, and resources.
4. **Use Visuals**: Pair your script with high-quality visuals and slides.
5. **Include a CTA**: Use a clear call-to-action for further engagement.
6. **Be Authentic**: Be honest and authentic in your script.
7. **Use a Clear Structure**: Use a clear structure to organize your content.
8. **Incorporate Humor**: Use humor if appropriate to engage your audience.
9. **Practice Timing**: Ensure your script is timed appropriately for the presentation length.

10. **Review and Revise**: Review and revise your script for clarity and impact.

DAY 96: STRATEGIES FOR INCREASING EMAIL OPEN RATES

Improving your email open rates is essential for successful email marketing campaigns. Here are strategies to boost your open rates:

1. **Craft Compelling Subject Lines**: Write engaging and curiosity-inducing subject lines.
2. **Personalize Emails**: Use the recipient's name and tailor content to their preferences.
3. **Segment Your List**: Group your audience based on behavior, demographics, or past interactions.
4. **Optimize Send Times**: Test and determine the best times to send emails to your audience.
5. **Use a Recognizable Sender Name**: Ensure your sender name is familiar and trustworthy.
6. **Keep It Mobile-Friendly**: Optimize your emails for mobile devices.
7. **Create a Sense of Urgency**: Use time-sensitive language to encourage immediate action.
8. **Test Different Elements**: A/B test subject lines, send

times, and email content.
9. **Avoid Spam Triggers**: Stay clear of spammy words and ensure your emails comply with spam regulations.
10. **Provide Value**: Ensure your emails offer valuable content that meets your audience's needs.

DAY 97: WRITING FOR VOICE SEARCH

Voice search is becoming increasingly popular, and optimizing your content for it can improve visibility. Here's how to write for voice search:

1. **Use Conversational Language**: Write in a natural, conversational tone.
2. **Focus on Long-Tail Keywords**: Use longer, more specific keywords that mimic natural speech.
3. **Answer Questions**: Structure content to answer common questions your audience might ask.
4. **Optimize for Local Search**: Include local keywords if your business targets a local audience.
5. **Keep It Simple**: Use simple sentences and straightforward language.
6. **Include Featured Snippets**: Aim to provide content that can be featured in snippets.
7. **Use Structured Data**: Implement schema markup to help search engines understand your content.
8. **Prioritize Mobile Optimization**: Ensure your website is mobile-friendly.
9. **Provide Clear Answers**: Offer clear and concise

answers to potential voice search queries.
10. **Regularly Update Content**: Keep your content up-to-date and relevant.

DAY 98: THE FUTURE OF COPYWRITING

The field of copywriting is constantly evolving. Here's a look at the future trends in copywriting:

1. **Increased Use of AI**: AI tools will continue to enhance and streamline the copywriting process.
2. **Personalization**: Highly personalized content will become even more critical.
3. **Interactive Content**: Interactive elements like quizzes, polls, and augmented reality will gain popularity.
4. **Voice Search Optimization**: Optimizing for voice search will be essential.
5. **Video Content**: Video scripts and video content will dominate the marketing landscape.
6. **Sustainability Messaging**: Emphasis on ethical and sustainable practices will increase.
7. **Augmented Reality**: AR will offer new ways to engage and interact with audiences.
8. **Data-Driven Copy**: Data and analytics will play a larger role in crafting and optimizing copy.

9. **Storytelling**: Authentic and compelling storytelling will continue to be a powerful tool.
10. **Cross-Channel Consistency**: Maintaining a consistent brand voice across all channels will be crucial.

DAY 99: WRITING FOR GLOBAL AUDIENCES

Writing for a global audience requires cultural sensitivity and awareness. Here's how to effectively write for a diverse audience:

1. **Understand Cultural Differences**: Research and respect cultural nuances and preferences.
2. **Use Clear Language**: Avoid slang, idioms, and jargon that may not translate well.
3. **Localize Content**: Adapt content to fit the cultural and linguistic context of each region.
4. **Be Mindful of Time Zones**: Consider time zones when scheduling communications.
5. **Use Universal Themes**: Focus on themes and messages that resonate universally.
6. **Test Translations**: Ensure translations accurately convey the intended message.
7. **Respect Legal and Ethical Standards**: Adhere to local laws and ethical standards.
8. **Incorporate Local Trends**: Stay updated with local trends and incorporate them into your content.
9. **Gather Feedback**: Seek feedback from native speakers

to ensure accuracy and appropriateness.
10. **Maintain Consistency**: Ensure your brand voice remains consistent across different languages and regions.

DAY 100: CONTINUOUS LEARNING AND IMPROVEMENT

The world of copywriting is dynamic, and continuous learning is key to staying ahead. Here's how to keep improving your copywriting skills:

1. **Stay Updated**: Follow industry blogs, news, and trends.
2. **Attend Workshops and Webinars**: Participate in events to learn from experts.
3. **Practice Regularly**: Write consistently to hone your skills.
4. **Seek Feedback**: Get feedback from peers, mentors, and your audience.
5. **Read Widely**: Read a variety of content to expose yourself to different styles and techniques.
6. **Analyze Successful Copy**: Study successful campaigns and content to understand what works.
7. **Experiment**: Try new techniques and approaches to

see what resonates with your audience.
8. **Take Courses**: Enroll in copywriting courses to learn new skills and strategies.
9. **Join Professional Groups**: Engage with copywriting communities and networks.
10. **Reflect and Adapt**: Regularly review your work, reflect on your progress, and adapt to new insights.

CONCLUSION

Mastering the art of copywriting is a journey that combines creativity, strategy, and continuous improvement. This eBook has covered a comprehensive range of topics, from understanding your audience and crafting compelling headlines to leveraging SEO techniques and adapting to the latest industry trends. By applying the principles and strategies outlined in these chapters, you can enhance your ability to write persuasive, engaging, and effective copy that resonates with your target audience.

In today's fast-paced digital world, the role of a copywriter is more important than ever. As you continue to develop your skills, remember to stay updated with industry changes, experiment with new techniques, and seek feedback to refine your craft. The future of copywriting is bright, with advancements in technology and evolving audience expectations presenting new opportunities to connect and communicate.

Whether you are writing for social media, email marketing, websites, or any other platform, the key is to stay true to your brand voice, provide value to your audience, and maintain a clear and compelling message. By doing so, you can build strong connections with your readers, drive conversions, and achieve your marketing goals.

Thank you for embarking on this journey through the world of copywriting. Keep practicing, stay curious, and continue learning. Your dedication to honing your skills will undoubtedly lead to success and recognition in the ever-evolving field of copywriting.

www.ingramcontent.com/pod-product-compliance
Lightning Source LLC
Chambersburg PA
CBHW071917210526
45479CB00002B/448